Descent, Ascent, Transfiguration

# Descent, Ascent, Transfiguration

Poems by
C. N. DUDEK

RESOURCE *Publications* · Eugene, Oregon

DESCENT, ASCENT, TRANSFIGURATION

Copyright © 2019 C. N. Dudek. All rights reserved. Except for brief quotations in critical publications or reviews, no part of this book may be reproduced in any manner without prior written permission from the publisher. Write: Permissions, Wipf and Stock Publishers, 199 W. 8th Ave., Suite 3, Eugene, OR 97401.

Resource Publications
An Imprint of Wipf and Stock Publishers
199 W. 8th Ave., Suite 3
Eugene, OR 97401

www.wipfandstock.com

PAPERBACK ISBN: 978-1-7252-5321-6
HARDCOVER ISBN: 978-1-7252-5322-3
EBOOK ISBN: 978-1-7252-5323-0

Manufactured in the U.S.A.                                                  11/11/19

*To*
*Primus Poeta*
*MARM*
*For always encouraging my poetry*
*MM, TO, J, C*
*K*

*Nessun maggior dolore che ricordarsi del tempo felice ne la miseria...*
—DANTE, *INFERNO* V.121–23

# Contents

**Book I: Descent**
Prelude: | 3
Fall | 5
I Once Did Dream | 6
Envy | 7
To Nietzsche | 8
Coleridge's Voyage | 10
Ms. S. Hutchinson | 11
The Seventh | 12
Across from the Market Tavern | 13
Hours | 15
A Depression | 16
Hel | 17
Joy | 18
Hidden | 19
untitled | 20
Ghost | 21
Golden Calf | 22
Shades | 23
Deception | 24
Odysseus | 25

**Book II: Ascent**
Orange Flame Atop Purgatory Grey | 29
Renaissance; Baroque | 30
The Lines on Our Faces | 31
Sea of Light | 32
Distressed Heart | 33

Bullet | 34
To Mary O'Connor | 35
Andalusia | 36
The Way of the Artist | 37
love | 38
Reformation | 40
River's Edge | 41
Night Sky | 42
Garden Wilderness | 43
Ember | 44
The Desert | 46
Books | 47
Bloom | 49
Dreams in Poiesis | 50

## Book III: Transfiguration

Dayflower | 55
Water Rapids | 56
Blue Waves | 57
7626 Miles | 58
Bare Behemoth Stone | 59
The World | 60
Kingdoms | 61
Survivor Tree | 62
Jormundgandr and the World Tree | 63
Baldur | 64
To J. R. R. Tolkien | 66
Friendship | 68
Ice | 69
December 2nd | 70
December 23rd | 71
Winter Wonder | 72
Ash Wednesday | 73
St. George's Day | 74
Mercy Sunday | 75
Trinity Sunday | 76
Babylon Forgotten | 78
untitled | 80

Remember in the Light of Your Love | 81
Silence | 82
beauty | 83
Foxes | 84
Pearl | 85
Upside Down | 87
Jewel; Icons | 89
Dusk | 90
Met with Joy | 91
Postlude: | 92

# Book I

# DESCENT

# Prelude

## To Dante

Beauty:

the allure, the goodness.
Beauty smiled on me
her gaze a beauteous glow.
The heart, the eyes tempted.
Pride rises—sin begetting sin
from the mind of disordered desire.
Desires twisted: covetous eyes, flesh.
Beauty becomes idol.
Effigy must be possessed.
The obsession.
loves disordered.

Restless.
We pine for someone, something
greater than Self
greater than It.
We desire Thou, but can only use It.
Seeing the world as It.
To be eaten,
to be consumed,
to be possessed.
Beauty is only beauty as Thou.

Then beauty becomes itself.
When the Good is our aim,
beauty becomes who she is—
her personality known, loved, and cherished.
Closer to God; becoming more human.
When God arrives, only then, the gods arrive.
The God of beauty, truth, goodness
making our desires His.
We see beauty as He sees.
To be loved, but more,

pointing toward Him,
Love that moves all things.

Beauty gazed upon my pale,
disheartened countenance.
My desires small, untempered.
Beauty turned her head, her gaze toward the fountain.
It was then I understood,
I too gazed upon the fountain
and saw the inviolable light.

**Fall**

The year almost over. The leaves crisping in the clear,

chill air.

My heart yearning with memory and loss. With what was and what might be. My blood, my heart slow. The sap in the trees do the same. Season nearing hibernation.

How does a broken heart mend? Over time?

How long?

"Though he fall, he shall not be utterly cast down: for the Lord upholds him with his hand." How does one build trust? How does one love again? How does . . .? "Wait for the Lord and keep his way . . ."

Cloud and wind destroy. Rains and tempests, wreck and dash to pieces, bodies and souls. "The Lord my light; my salvation . . ."

Depths of the ocean within the eyes, the wisdom of the galaxies. "Teach me your way, O Lord, and lead me on a level path." The soul burns to rise, but weighed down by its vice. Learn from the falling leaves and the burning fires. A quiet in the embers and rising heat.

"To you, O Lord, I call; my rock, be not deaf to me . . ." Seeking you in all things. But forgetting the first, like Gomer. "Seek ye first . . ." Yearning for stability and life and love and wholeness again. Two lost. Only You save. But what of the role of the Beatrice-figure?

"I cried to you for help, and you have healed me. O Lord, you have brought up my soul from Sheol . . ." My person grows dim. A gray soul, a pale body. Kneeling, making self small.

After the long winter, after a long death Persephone brings blooms of life, from gray to color. The color rising within me. Divine love bringing all things, beings, creatures to life. The God of love, justice, mercy, grace upholding all things, renewing all, making all things whole, all things new.

The leaves turn brilliant burning colors before they die. So I follow the archetype. And fall with the leaves. Shattering, heart breaking to be remade. The image of God searing through.

**I Once Did Dream**

O what a dream I once did dream
of skies blue and crystal lakes,
each morning a delight,
existential dread unknown.

A dream where joy resides,
ocean breezes, blue on blue
ever extending.
Where a person is not a savior
content in anyone's company.
Loneliness unheard of . . .

O what a dream I once did dream,
a dream to be
a dream once dreamed.

## Envy

Envy, a poison

muting love of neighbor

our discontents manifest in grumbling over what others have

a melancholy mixed in the heart that murders neighbor;

glee at another's downfall.

Envy derived from pride—the root of all discontents.

Bemoan the envy that poisons yourself and others.

Live wisely, within the gifts given and content with what is given.

Heed the call of who *you* are; not anyone else.

Envy poisons our thoughts and lives.

Ruminate in the truth; the God who is love—

not in love. Love is not God.

But the God, who is love redeems all the others.

That envy and other maladies are put in their place—

all in right order.

## To Nietzsche

Early Greek dichotomy:
born of chaos brought to order;
life is suffering.

Embrace that there is no salvation from suffering;
loss and mortality: repair not, reform not, transcend not.
Death is the way; fate, power—accept your fate.
No wonder Nietzsche used the pagan Greek view—
nihilism as fatalism.

Nihilism the destruction of our age—
no need for meaning or reasonable living.
It more palatable than redemption, as Wendell has said.

Yet the tension lies within—
we humans beat against the nihilistic machine
melancholy and pain, suffering awakening our senses
this is not all there is—
pain and suffering make no sense,
but to embrace in the light of Christ's suffering
brings it to bearing.

Black and white dichotomy:
light and dark;
order and chaos
too simple an explanation for complex human living
world created by complex, loving, unknowable,
yet knowable in Christ.
The world a wonder—to be adored, pointing toward its Maker.

God created good; not evil.
Through a fallen world, the light of Christ shines through
even the bleakest vision can be transformed
changing one's philosophy—
to an embracing of the Creator's love of His creation.

Apollo and Dionysius are dead,
never existed or put to right order.

Away! Nihilism.
The God of truth, beauty and goodness put all things aright,
instilling wonder and love; His mark in all His creation
in the hearts of His image.
Chiaroscuro no longer, but full color.

## Coleridge's Voyage

Lifeless in a world of ice.

Plying through icy sludge, a water looks heavy

A killing chill

Fear to plunge beneath, never to return from dark blackness, depths.

Lifeless, alone, nearing despair.

The lifeless ice stiffening the life of the traveler.

Before nearing despairing death,

a wide-winged albatross appears.

Life carried within, to buoy the despairing.

The Mariner shot the life, nearly destroying himself,

stabbing to the heart of his soul,

yet a death may lead one to resurrection.

Instead of the cross around the neck, the albatross

As he plies the lonely frozen waters.

## Ms. S. Hutchinson

The Muse to lift the melancholy spirit of the poet.
Verse soaring to heights long forgotten
A bursting of the heart in rapturous joy.
The Muse lifting from despair
But deeper despair soon to follow.
One's own arrow piercing the heart of beloved
comes crashing down,
a pain worse than former anguish.

The heart clings, unwilling to fully let go.
Heart in pain, an anguish like a fire of hell.
But the fire, God's love disguised.

The speed of mercy, severe—
transfiguration its goal.
Purgation like a hell,
but union with Love
Truth, Beauty
its true goal.

Death its consequence, but death to self
to be raised again—God the aim.

To know thyself
is to know weaknesses,
owning one's self-deceived heart
knowing its suffering brought by disordering
will
sin: bringer of death,
But God is near even in mark missed—
through suffering, renewal—transfiguring
after the long, painful, excruciating voyage.

## The Seventh

Proverbs 5:1–20

Who am I but a wretched man?
Who but one who has broken vows . . .
What is in your heart will be made known.
Hidden within will only brittle your bones
and weaken flesh.
To will one thing is purity of heart.
The heart broken
shattered into pieces . . .

Unclean am I . . .
Touch the coal to my lips
to my heart . . . be made clean
as hoarfrost.
saint within the wretch:
Kichijiro
Only You can save.

heart broken,
seeking one to save;
stuffing it with temporal things,
masking pain.
Save her
That she may enter the kingdom;
made whole.
Sorrow and brokenness and sin washed away.
Rend our hearts—
You, a merciful God who loves mankind.
Do not be wrath with us.
Teach her your ways.
Jesus, remember me,
remember her in your kingdom.

## Across from the Market Tavern

Where I broke down
with sobs of turpitude.
Lies breaking nerve.
Nervous breakdown?

Tears of remorse like waters of lament
forming rivers and streams
watering the world in abundance.
Journal to write, but mind in fog
hands could not coordinate.
The journal like a fortress on an island I could not reach, but was my salvation.
In darkness and cold, weeping.

Vulnerable heart taken advantage of;
kind disposition easily manipulated.
Disposition, Ha! What virtues can save? None.
Crass creatures we are. The only capable of such lamentable behavior.
Murder in my heart, killing memory only for a deluge of suppressed emotion to spill over.
Autumn brings out murdered memory,
reminiscence that pains the intellect and the broken body.
Nothing suppressing memory and former action. Sedation and escape.
One only makes meaning of suffering. The broken body on the rough wooden cross.
The grotesque body saving all the world, all the cosmos; all within it.

Ghosts haunting the psyche,
apparitions flitting before my eyes. Ghosts my memories of better times.
In purgatory, I am a ghost purgated; pain the redemption.
Severe the mercy.
But leads to glory.
How long, O Lord?
Wash me in the river where good memory remains, but the memory of sin forgotten forever.
I am the ghost awaiting full reality, solid again, body; soul, whole being.
Waiting for the image to be restored.

The parking lot, the place of hitting bottom;
across from the market tavern, where other ghosts drank with jollity and friends.
I, alone, solitude amongst the crowd. Deserved isolation in my melancholy.

Two years passed. Canine companion has helped alleviate lonesomeness. "It is not good for man to be alone." No companion was fit for the man of dust, except that made from his own flesh. Longing for flesh of my flesh, but canine will do for now. There is joy in God's small creatures.

A train calls in the distance. A journal my solace.

## Hours

Between the hours of four and five
Between the sun and the moon
Birds sing in joy or
sing a dirge
To purge the melancholy
from the mist
That clouds despairingly.
Hoping for death
the setting sun.
But the sun soon to rise.
To burn away the dew
tears left behind.
Losing mind
and soul sinking into the
rolling mist.

The heart a fist,
only love's divine hand
can unfist.

## A Depression

Depression,
like the hidden caverns of water under the earth . . .
As much water under the earth as above.
A lava flow boiling pitch hidden
seeping to the surface.
Water and fire collide,
creating a bastion
like the gray walls of Dis.

Liturgy of isolation, fear,
leading to madness, darkness.
Stagnant waters and dark, cold places.

Things hidden exposed to the light,
the dinge; the dirt,
stagnation
cleansed with brightness, water and fire.
What once built walls of silence
and silent, dark holes,
now embraces breezes
and moving, cleansing waters
burning with purifying fires.

Depression, nearly leading to frozen lakes of Cocytus.
Dying in frozen stink.
But the piercing light opens paths
long forgotten.
The walls of Dis no longer standing, only ruins
lost in darkness.

## Hel

Loki had a daughter named Hel.

Odin brought her to the deepest, darkest part under the earth and made her queen.

Those who died in childbirth, old age, in their sleep, all manner of death besides those of battle came to her in the darkest part of the earth.

In darkness—darkness their home. No light. No light of hope.

Light of life, absent.

The Greeks have Hades.

Those who died, disembodied and decaying.

Hel: a half smile with dead eyes, rotting flesh; decaying soul.

No hope for an embodied existence again.

A place of death that has no hope for life again. A mass of shades.

The chains of death bound the dead for all time.

Until the end of the world. One harrowed this place of death.

One who died and conquered death by death.

The one resurrected into fullness of life; gives hope of this life to us mortals.

Only the gods would live again—but the Son of God makes mortals like God that we may live again.

No longer bound to darkness or death. Only light and life. Ablaze with hope.

## Joy

Joy
elusive joy
joy in appetite? never lasting
the happiness from thing to thing . . .
elusive and never ending.
In the search for happiness, it is missed and never attained.
Fleeting moments and brief timespans
it clings to us
But never lasts. Temporary appeasement.
Joy only found eternal and lasting from One source.
All else is substitute.

## Hidden

Joy like the sun
brightening mood, like innocent love
that lifts the heart.

But it is dark.
Joy is hidden beneath layers of shame.
Shame dimming all vision to see.
Music lifts, fine arts, blue sky
but a bright sun is missing
that joy and levity
making footsteps light and free.
Feeling forsaken, deserted, abandoned
yet,
"I will always be with you,"
Even in the darkness.
Truth ever-present.

The sun behind the clouds; night perpetual.
Winter . . .

**untitled**

Lonely soul

in a record shop.

The warm tones

from a spinning pressed vinyl

fills an empty space

like light.

Plastic, cardboard and vinyl

tangible—

a comfort.

He leaves,

a small presence resides inside,

but still walks alone

in silence—

upon the uneven brick pavement.

# Ghost

Wandering with no direction

running from pain

and misguided affections.

Roaming in melancholy

twisted.

The knife cannot

cut that which is

guazy and immaterial.

Cannot bleed

the broken, wizened heart.

All the things that made me real

I burned

but I'm not even a flame

roaming the earth.

A cold transparency.

Disquiet wearing away the soul.

Searching and seeking things that cannot make me solid again.

## Golden Calf

Golden calf, red calf

Our golden idols we hold high
atop high places.
Lofting our elusive happiness high.
Golden shackles; our wills free to choose

destruction.

Until the red calf comes
ushering in the Finality of all things.
A justice never seen.
Perfection present
to our lofted sins.

Like ash we become
unless we turn away from iniquity
at the arrival of the red calf.

In the meantime, the golden calf,
the idol we worship.
Guised in happiness
dealings with ourselves and others numbed
loving ourselves despite others.

"Love your neighbor as long as it serves Self."
This is the golden calf's mantra.

But the red calf comes.

Our fantasy of happiness burned away with Reality.
Love's consuming fire. A presence only saints can withstand. Just barely.

## Shades

In Hades I find myself.
I slit the throat of the goat
its blood spills upon the dark soil.
Shades appear like stippled photographs
Lapping up the blood.
I should have slit my own throat, I think.
But then I would be dead among the dead.
Trapped in my mind, as a shade for eternity
reaping what I sowed, seeping blood into the soil that will only produce
a stillborn soul.

Body hanging separate like rotted fruit from the soul's branches.
I want to live amongst the living,
but misery brings me to the shores of putrid rivers
of stinking muck.

The shades do not comfort.
They do not pray.
They only go on in hopelessness.
Trapped within their minds; within their regrets and passions.
Unrepentant and spoiled.

Hades the land of the dead. Never to be reborn.
I search for Proserpine. But she has already left
to rouse earth's blooms.
Lost in the darkness.

The Gorgon appears petrifying me in despair.
How can this nightmare end?
The earth quakes beneath me. A rift in the crust. A light shines through.

Shades, Gorgons flee.
Here is my hope, my savior—
Come down to set captives free.

## Deception

With the return of melancholy

while weaning from sedative soma

creativity has slowly returned.

Though dizziness from sickness will make this a fragmentary, baroque work.

***

I have been Saul persecuting Christ; thrown from the horse of pride. Blinded. Converted.

Hosea the cuckolded crying for fidelity. But also Gomer with wandering heart. Unfaithful.

David and Bathsheba. Blinded by passion, justifying with mental gymnastics. Until confronted by Nathaniel.

My name a paradox, romantic courts of flirtation, courting, sometimes infidelity. Second name the prophet who confronts David, causing him to repent. They lose the child born of infidelity.

Tartuffe the deceiver, yet those enamored by him are deceived by themselves. Princesse de Cleves, "we are very weak when we are in love."

Lose our minds. Infidelity very much the Pit Proverbs speaks about.

To divide the heart destroys. Some can play the game, but I cannot. Compartmentalization is not a strength of mine, which is honorable.

Being used and discarded for others a disgrace. Lied to—beyond the description of pain. Strung along. Taken advantage of . . . with no self-respect. Deadly combination.

Suicide an option for several years or just hoping to not wake the next day or not caring if something terrible happened. A fictional character created who pledged self-murder March 17th, luckily those days have been surpassed.

Through the mess and self-destruction—grace still present. The God of restoration and light and life–the ever-faithful—present always and forever.

## Odysseus

Ino save me from the
tumultuous waves.

The crashing swells
toiling, drowning
waters.

Wrap me in your veil
that no water
may drown me.
None but waters of renewal.

# Book II

# ASCENT

## Orange Flame Atop Purgatory Grey

Virgil gird the waste with water reed,
Cleanse the face from Hell's dross.
Purging fire;
joy in sorrow.
Cato rebukes souls for tarrying.

Ascent must begin
Moving toward pinnacle-garden
Passing through flame.
Grace urges soul to ascend
Melting sin: pride, envy, wrath, sloth, lust
Like dross from silver refined.

Lethe and Eunoe to wash away memory of sin;
restoring anamnesis; good deeds done.
Stricken for straying
Repentant pilgrim
Baptized in waters of Eunoe
Ready for the stars.

## Renaissance; Baroque

Renaissance heart; baroque emotions

Desire order and beauty that points toward divine
yet emotions wild–untempered desire.

Brightness vivid color;
yet dark tones of melancholy
a swampy mist covering all the world.
Dimming eyes, minds, vision blurred.

The uncertain world stained with nihilism;
bright vivid colors of the Renaissance remind

of brilliance, of illuminated images

of God burning within each icon

of the grotesque, yet divine human image.

## The Lines on Our Faces

the lines on our faces
like rings within a tree;
lines on the trunks and rough bark.
Telling stories of storms. Growth.
Brokenness, where wounds were but now healed.
Silent marks telling a lifetime.
Weather-worn skin speaking without saying a word.
the lines on our faces
telling tales:
life, suffering, pain.

## Sea of Light

moon reflects upon the sea
cresting waves crash
a sound of hope
unique unto itself.

stars in the inky dark:
sky and waters,
light of a thousand years past
not knowing the darkness of our soul.

But light— O glorious light
purify and reflect upon moving,
cleansing waters—crashing
restoring my soul; all souls.

## Distressed Heart

dispirited: the thorn,

dogma of outside the purview of grace,

seems more a myth.

The speed of grace a violence,

an assault narrowing the focus

of the prodigal, the one who has lost the way.

Sin, the punishment.

This journey of life a hardship,

dragons line the road, wills in contention.

Yet in toil, grace abounds.

The heart must turn or keep its course of self-destruction.

Eventually weariness, the grace.

God: ever the hound of heaven seeking his beloveds.

Flannery said it well, we breathe nihilism daily; it is everywhere.

Let melancholy, hardship be the grace that turns the battered heart toward the steadfast God

who loves us with all His being—

His being is Love.

Take not the Spirit; His love endures forever.

The burning coal; fire of love, a distress that heals.

## Bullet

speed of mercy*
a bullet
splitting through
self-deception and complacency.
Sentimental and decorous language need not apply.
Christ the Tyger, Tyger burning bright**
severity of God's divine love.
Gentle Jesus, a farce.

With all of our being, we resist redemption
and hope for the best.
But the bullet of grace is what turns our ways.
The prophetic speech, God's burning love shot through
to turn our stubborn sensibilities
as we walk through the valley of death
where dragons line the roads threatening to devour.

In the eleventh hour,
through suffering, we turn back
God's face shining, facing us.
Our heart abandoned, but He never left.
The haunting shadow eternally present.
Leading us toward teleologic shalom.

---

\* phrase from Baron von Hugal
\*\* from William Blake

# To Mary O'Connor

Born the feast of the Annunciation
a voice, shocking each
revealing blindness and sin
within pious facade.
Reminding reader
bent toward self.
Shocking out of complacency
and myopia,
This cancerous self-deception.

A voice against nihilism and judgmentalism.
She shows us our own hearts,
proclaiming to love,
each person presented to us.
Though they may smell,
be annoying, despise you, be bothersome.
Reminding the reader of great importance: this frail, fragile body.
That the Savior came in the same grotesque, smelling, dirty body.
Not a clean, pious, detached savior,
but one of our own afflictions, sharing in our frailty.
Not a spiritual savior, but a real,
human being, yet paradoxically God.

But in his humanness many missed that he was also fully divine.
Flannery reminding, we are not Gnostics,
but the Savior was born through blood and water.
Messy, disgusting, beautiful life.
To see the world as it was meant to be seen:
natural world infused with the divine.

## Andalusia

To live under a fourteen-year death
Sentence, creates poignant beloved stories.
Routine of writing; Mass beforehand.
To see the world through divine vision.

Eyes as blue as the peacock's neck,
Like an angel of God, piercing the darkened
Heart that beats within our chest that no one knows.
Rain pours to cleanse a darkened mind running
To the crimson river looking for the
Kingdom of God as the red sun sets
Like a bloodied host and conscience knocked about.

The green fields viewed from the porch in Georgia heat,
A setting bringing her characters to life.
Typing tales then throwing them away.
After publication, Regina
Retrieving them from the trash as though scraps.

Fourteen years suffering to create Master works.
Life in absence of suffering seems a joke.
A shock of grace always penetrates
This deaf and blinded world to see the vision
Like the green and blue of the peacock
Displaying his eyes like stars, pointing
To the one who redeemed suffering.

Andalusia in green-fielded Georgia
Opens the dimming eyes to see grace
In nearly all things.

## The Way of the Artist

To go the way of van Gogh,
breathing in the beauty of life and light,
yet a lonely, melancholy genius
that wracked the whole of his being
plunging him into despair, though beauty shined all around him.
Beauty his Muse, the way of the artist
peaks and pits of emotion—
creating wonders.

Shot through with melancholy
God only knows what brings one to deepest pits of despair . . .
Only the God of mercy knows the plight of the suicide—
Life a gift not easily taken.
Madness derails senses and reason—
melancholy a powerful fury ready to snip the chord hanging over the head
plunging into darkness
the open maw decrying life.

To go the way of van Gogh,
the way of the sensitive soul,
the way of the artist;
sensitive and fragile—
a cross to carry,
a place to tread lightly, compassionately, cautiously.
What grace; what mercy might the God of life have for the suicide?
A question to ponder carefully; with much
wisdom,
time,
delicacy.

## love

Flickering flames
igniting other souls,
koinonia
cultivating one another.
Divine grace—
love the impetus.

Displaced from the flames
the wick burns quickly
a weak heat remains,
Nearly extinguished.
Hope resides in community.

Alone and aloof—
despair sets in.

The world breaks our heart
we break our own
making cordis like stone.
God gives affliction and consolation—both His will.
Only the Great Physician
heals and makes the heart flesh again.
Nurture the flame. Otherwise it will blow out.
Becoming a ghost—lost and wandering.

Haunting the body
pushing all away—
even love
leaving our heart
cold, solid like
Cocytus perpetually
frozen.
No movement—
only despair
a gnawing at the
back of the mind.

Gathered fire
only melts the ice—
fire of God's love
grace.

**Reformation**

If only the rain
brought solace.
If only I were alive.
If only the pain
had meaning and grace.

Blue skies
and blue waters
and an embrace
to cease pain and shame.

Rain pelts down
to drown sorrow
to wash away
burdens and blame.

Take this suffering
and renew the face,
the shattered life
with grace
and fire.

Blue skies and waters,
silence in deserts,
splendid sunsets
canyons, heights, rushing rivers
waterfalls;
painted deserts.
Beauteous creation
reminders of reformation.

## River's Edge

I fell asleep at the river's edge
in the rain and cloud.
As the river tumbled down.
I dreamed a dream
unmarked by time.
memories, people, places,
of Gilead.
A restful dream.
But I awoke to cloud and rain
and time flowing on.
I awoke to sadness
yet a peace resided deep
within.
As though the river left
me something as I
dreamed
by the river's edge.

**Night Sky**

Crisp, cold, cloudless sky
illuminating moon
planet beside.
Signs silent in the night sky
declaring nothing
Season of discontents.

All the world's Your stage,
but I see nothing,
but what the modern sees.
What a tragedy.

Pierce my eyes with illuminating lights
of celestial stars and planetae.
Round moon's face—grace.

The sun rising the next day.

## Garden Wilderness

Wilderness—

parched, dried land,

cracked, chasms thirsting,

weeds thrive,

flowers die.

The broken sinner

limps among the weeds,

thirsting in the wilderness.

But lo, a voice cries in the wilderness.

"Salvation is near."

Sinner thirsts in unison with the land.

Baptismal river snakes through arid acres.

Land fraught with Temptation, despair, wretchedness.

The church in wilderness.

It is not a beautiful garden.

The people are in wilderness, yearning for the garden.

The shepherd in the desert points the way.

## Ember

Filling melancholy days
with melancholy tones.
Ice grips the heart
freezing my bones.
I need the warmth
of perfect love—
which only One provides.
But all is silent
a darkness shrouding—
yet a little flame,
well, really an ember
hiding amongst the ash.
Motion and movement keeps alive.

Ice threatens to kill.

If "every thought is a thought of You" then is Your thought of me
sustaining

my being?

Though melancholic ice
stiffens and nearly extinguishes.
I can't trust myself
Ice flowing in my veins.

Warmth of the Good, of Love—
a heat felt, though distant.
The image still present,
badly damaged.
Fan the ember
with that which moves all things—
a consuming fire.

As the light fades and cold sets in
only the warmth of Love divine
keeps alive
though not felt or seen—

ever-present,
Even in the melancholic
shroud of a cold heart, blind and unfeeling.

## The Desert

The desert's silence,

the endless horizon.

The painted sands.

Reds, oxides, browns, white, ignatius rock.

Pictographs. Revealing hidden things.

You cannot hide your self in the desert.

Arid.

Cliffs and plateaus. No strength to climb.

Mirages. Burning thirst. Unsatiated.

Brisk the morning; scorching midday.

Spirits in the undulating waves of heat against painted sands.

Promising with empty hands and sands cascading through fingers.

No friends to be found.

Only temptation that promises more than what can actually be given.

Promising emptiness—impossible fulfillment.

After wandering for years, a tuft of chartreuse prairie grass seen ahead.

And a golden sunset amidst gray cloud.

## Books

Books in a room
on shelves
on the floor
cascading like steps.
Some open
others closed—
torn pages
pages burned
pages missing.
Some books stabbed through.
All the words
of joy, heartache,
loss,
love,
hard-heartedness,
death and life.

Melancholy.

This wonderful life.

This painful, suffering life.

Obscure titles.
Others well known.
All words of this hurting, painful world.
Books on tables
on chairs.

Cracked spines—

browning pages—

A room—

filled with

the soul's pages.

## Bloom

Rigid, narrow-visioned.
Frozen, cold
hardened ice,
face etched from marble
stone features.
Heart hardened. Words and emotion break against it
like waves against rocky shores.

Wildness, the fall from such height,
breaks upon rock's immovable face
shattering most of what was known.
All he can do is stare into the pool of glassy water.
Broken apart, cursed . . .

But in the emptiness, in the wandering, a seed planted
and white and yellow daisies bloom along the path
of his wandering journey.

## Dreams in Poiesis

*O Holy City of the East. I miss your ancient stories told in the white rock. The mountains of war, blasphemy, peace, transformation and yearning for the Promised Land. Where Christ stepped, I and we stepped. We met on the beach of Galilee. "Feed my sheep."*

*We met and were fed by the miracle of the fish and bread. We were taught the "Our Father" and the Beatitudes.*

*We betrayed Christ and affirmed our love for Him.*

*We built the high places, but allowed Him to tear them down.*

*We smote the priests of Baal with Elijah on Mt. Carmel, witnessing God's wrath toward sin.*

*We walked the streets of Jerusalem in sorrow and adoration. Surrounded by olive trees and whispers of olive presses, we prayed with Christ in His agony. Finally, we touched Golgotha, the mount of sacrifice.*

*Heaven meets earth in those places. It is beautiful agony. I am with you until the end of the age. Coming in the clouds. (2010)*

While I lived at home in 2004, in exile from the world, cloistered in the woods of New Jersey, I had a vivid dream. I was in Jerusalem. I walked in a dry and hot place. It was nearing evening, but the sky was red. I walked a path toward a city. But devils were taunting me; wicked-looking children with grotesque faces. When they touched me, they seared my skin. I came to a graveyard. In part of the dream I was Mary, the mother of Jesus. Toward the end of the dream I was myself. I walked amongst the tombstones. They were all lying flat on the ground. I was walking in circles and stepping on the stones. I stopped on a stone that had an icon of Mary on it. Then I was in the present and weeping because my father was dying or I was dying (in reality, my father was dying of cancer). I wanted to tell a friend what was going on, but he was sleeping. I wanted others to understand my pain and my sorrow.

Looking back, some things come to light. The Garden of Gethsemane. Jesus wept and was in agony, sweating blood asking for this cup to pass. When I was with my dad in New Jersey, some of my friends slept while I prayed and was in agony. I wanted the cup of sorrow and stress and a journey of pain to pass, but I accepted God's will. The sky red and the heat may have represented the strife of my soul, nearing despair. It seemed like despair, but it was a purgation in the dark night of the soul. The red representing the light of Jupiter, joviality, joy, a kingly presence. Though I was in a desert, spiritually and physically spent, the king of life was in the midst of my sorrow. My tongue tasting only dust. My bones peeking through flesh. Heaviness upon my shoulders. The king of joy was present through suffering. Though suffering spends the night, joy comes in the morning. I was mourning myself in the dream, dying to myself. Death comes physically, but death also comes when we choose Christ; we die with him in the water and rise with him. Baptism. The old man (Adam) dies in us, daily. We rise with Christ, the new Adam. We are rising as new creatures in Christ. The blood moon, the red-stained sky. It is the end of ourselves. That we may rise with the King of life in the New Jerusalem. The City of Eternal Life where with the saints, Mary and the King, Jesus Christ reigns eternal. We rejoice after the long road of suffering and divine love. With all the company of heaven, we live bodily where time no longer exists. But only true Reality with the true God.

The New Jerusalem will be home. While we are in exile here, we see glimpses of the remade world, how things should have been, despite the Fall. We long for home. We long for the cosmos to be remade. It has been, it is, and it will be remade. The world died at the cross. Christ is the life of the world and the world killed him. At Christ's bodily resurrection, the world is being remade. As the Church, we work with God to remake it. We gratefully accept it, but we give it back to God that He may redeem it. The world cannot be remade, but by Christ. This sounds contradictory. But those who are followers of Christ are the ones in Christ carrying on the mission of Christ. This is not utopia-building, but the Kingdom of God. For God has the final say; it is His kingdom. We are those forgiven and being perfected to trod among the saints with Christ. God is our end. Our desires transformed by Christ in his grace to love the good, to love God, to desire to be perfect as our heavenly Father is perfect. Only by Christ, in Christ can this happen. He is our life and our perfection. Lord, purge me of impurity. Give me purity of heart, humility, a hunger for your righteousness, and your grace to do these. To see your face.

# Book III

# TRANSFIGURATION

## Dayflower

Asiatic dayflower
blooms for a day and fades with setting sun.
Azure like cloudless sky
In the cool morning, blue pops through green
like stars in a black canopy.
A calming blue through calming green
a peace settles in the morning breezes
to meet a day of calamity.
Asiatic dayflower
here for a day; gone by evening,
but to return in the morning.

## Water Rapids

I wait with the stillness of the blue heron.

Amidst the rushing rapids. The water whirling and churning white.

Speak to me Lord, amidst the roar of the Waters. With blue heron waiting with one purpose. Silently waiting.

In a moment, the sun illuminates the water. Waiting for the light at the right time to capture the beauty of creation.

Sun, cloud covered, suddenly bright as though His presence announced. I see You, but still do not hear you. Your beauty everywhere.

I stand in the rushing water just behind the heron.

Watching the unstoppable water find its way down the rocks to the pooling water below.

Searching for meaning, but unable to make sense of what is around me. May be God telling me to be still and delight in everything He has brought before me. The rocks, water, trees, fish, minnows the heron eats carried down in the rapids; the heron, light, sun, the winds.

His highest creation, fellow humans.

I could not hear Him in the sounds of the rushing Waters.

But only in the silence of golden light.

## Blue Waves

The blue Pacific beckons to me—

calling in the night—the quiet, dismal light.

Not a Siren's call, but a call to contemplation

a tranquil, purposed leisure—that remakes, renews.

The cold blue waters, sobering–awakening the wreaked soul within.

Pulling from the depths that which was lost and salvaging the good and piecing it back together again.

Drowning in the frigid waters is lifesaving. Only one God can bring the dead back to life.

The Pacific blue beckons me to its roar and crashing upon seashore.

Cresting swells and renewing waters. Not chasing each wave, but setting out to sea, to the hope beyond the horizon.

**7626 Miles**

Seven thousand six hundred twenty-six miles
to leave lassitude behind.
Seek the divine
in music.
Silence in the desert. Zion in the canyons.
Where seraphim land amidst the yellow and red rock—
painted landscapes.
The roar of the Pacific against white sands.
Azure waters crash against cliff and rock.

Leaving lassitude behind.

Gas lamp
and French Quarter;
Jackson Park; mighty Mississippi
churning.
Yellow-flowered fields.
Forest of the giants reaching;
crystal forests long dead.
Wyoming skies, cold low-lying ceiling clouds.
Misty, snow-capped mountains.
Glorious stars,
sunrise and sunset atop the mountains.

Leaving lassitude behind.

Roaring fires and winds stirring desert sands blocking serene skies.
Orange groves, windmills powering cities in the night.
Oklahoma sunset yellow-bleeding sky.
Navajo, Hopi, Hualapai selling wares near the grandest of canyons.

Seven thousand six hundred twenty-six miles to leave lassitude behind.

## Bare Behemoth Stone

The bare gray-stone behemoth
the mountain endures
weather, rain, snow;
nature never lies.

Constant: it is what
it always is
gray solid rock.
Never searching.
It knows its existence
and creator.
The war within absent.

Gray rock against
blue
sky.
Ever looking upward.

## The World

In all its splendor, majesty and beauty; color and form,
mountains, rivers; blues and greens.
Flowers, plains, oceans;
atmospheric splendor.
Gems in luminous color—to dazzle the eye.
Created Good.

But there is another world. It lies in evil. In darkness. The world Jesus did not want to pray for.
The kingdom of the Prince of this world.
The perversion of the created order. The activities of men that hurt, destroy.
Gratify the eye, corrupt nature, the pomp of life.
Atomic bombs and lust-filled intent.
Secrets of the heart that no one knows.
An ambition to dominate and conquer all things in man's image.
Consume and use all. The world of the darkened heart—influenced by the Prince of the dark.

On the Last Day the world began its transformation, but it is not complete.
The darkness has yet to be brought to justice, to its rightful end.
Easter has begun with incarnation and resurrection, but the culmination of all things remains.

**Kingdoms**
(written on 9/11/2018)

Breaking news—murder,
political scandal, bomb, massacre, war, espionage, controversial speech.
The despondent world.
Inundates psyche.
Hopelessness its song.

Good news—
a Savior was born
in Bethlehem
amidst death, war,
and turmoil.
He was killed
but rose again and will come again
to judge the living and the dead.

The Savior gathers these
broken pieces;
we remember
what was and what is to come.
Hope—the song.

## Survivor Tree

I sit in silence before the survivor tree.

Where over a decade ago, death surrounded it.

Nearly crushed by tons of steel, drywall; bodies, corpses turned to dust.

Like love, it stands tall and unmoved

Though the play of death and tragedy performed and continues an encore.

Death lacks strength enough to flood,

to quench,

to destroy the Love that upholds all things.

Death lacks the final say.

The tree lives on,

its seed taken across the country,

the world

planted elsewhere.

Life continues, though death so near.

Symbol of eternal life that Love carries onward.

Reminder of hope though set in the crucible of an unrelenting world.

## Jormundgandr and the World Tree

It feels like the division within is much like Loki's daughter—Hel.

One side, decaying, dead, a withered eye, flesh decrepit as though hung from a tree for weeks or frozen in the snow and bitter cold.

The other side brimming with life, pink, blood flowing, feeling blood flow within. The vivid green eye glimmering like a jewel.

It feels like Jormundgandr poisons life and burns living flesh that yearns to live and thrive. Pressed between stones unable to move, the poison dripping, burning.

A part yearns to live; the other wishes to die, ending suffering and misery. A loathed dichotomy, Nietzschean in design.

But the world tree lives on. The tree of life.

Not life reoccurring in cycle, but continuing on forever, world without end.

Death will be destroyed once and for all. The yearning for death no longer present, not even a flicker of a thought. The "game of the gods" will not continue. But a union and life in full will be.

The half-dead smile of Hel will no longer be. Only those fully alive present. Can Hel be made whole? Or will it be destroyed forever? The second death of those brought to justice. Hel does not know, neither Jormundgandr nor Loki, the all-Father;

the Trinity may.

But we mortals can only hope that Hell will be empty at Ragnarok. The end of all things.

As some live divided lives—heaven and hell battling within—the poison of Jormundgandr burning and blinding, the dead half of Hel awaits your death, but does her living side hope for your eternal life?

She declared Baldur was the most beautiful thing in her kingdom and wished to keep him, though no blood flowed in his veins. His skin pale and dead. Within Hel's green eye, did she imagine the pulsing life of Baldur returning to him? Did she witness the Christ, a living man, storm her gate like Frigg? Yet Christ was able to bring those dead back to the land of the living. The kingdom of death unraveling.

The promise of the tree of life. That death would not reign for eternity.

## Baldur

Baldur the beautiful is dead
is dead.

Nothing in all of creation would kill Baldur—
not disease, stone, metal, weapon—anything
but one: Mistletoe. The parasitic plant clinging to trees.
Baldur's brother tricked by Loki to fashion a dart of mistletoe
expecting it to do no harm.

But the dart slew Baldur. All the world wept his death.
Every rock, tree, even the metals in the earth wept.
Every animal—every creature, every god. But one: Loki.

Baldur sojourned to the land of the dead, Hel's kingdom where there was
no dawn.
She thought him the most beautiful creature as everything and everyone
did.

All the world trembled at his loss in the land of the living.
The gods sought to retrieve him from the kingdom of the dead, but failed.

Only one as wise and adored (by some, a paradox) would break the chains
of Hel's kingdom.
Life itself sacrificed for the Life of the world. Life slain that all may live again. A rune written before the worlds were made, a promise from before the beginning kept and fulfilled. Written in the earth. Written in the cosmos. The death of God to redeem the world and all in it. All that wept for him and all that despised him.

The dawn finally came to those in Hel's kingdom. His flesh was not gray or white or green or blue. But life pulsed within. That the dead may live again. On that first Easter morn, the dawn pierced the land of the dead—
hope rising where it had never been.
Baldur was beloved, but could not live again even with the gods' power.

But the Son of God would rise again and the dead in his train, rising with him, no longer pale ghosts, but made whole.
Baldur the beautiful is dead,
is dead.

But all will rise again,
again.

## To J. R. R. Tolkien

Imagination forged in ice
Of the Norse,
Turmoil, war, suffering.
The Somme in his bones
like Norse giants causing
Catastrophe, victory, doom, honor.
Imagination steeped in classics,
wonder of nature:
beauty and peace. Deep roots of green trees,
sap flowing.
Magic of life pulsing within.
The cascading power of rivers Ever-flowing over rock.
A musical rhythm Telling of the old world,
yet dark Doom emerging through black wood,
from the depths of Misty Mountains.

Deep roots of the mountains
And trees,
thousands of years, awash within characters' memories.
Evil rearing its hydra head, Destruction its aim.
But the eucatastrophe,
The smallest, insignificant, unnoticed thing
desolates destructive force, rendering evil impotent.

Bombadil, the first man
Singing joyously through wood saving hobbits from barrows
Transforming them into wraiths.
The Ents guardians of the forests,
As old as the earth itself.
Timeless undying, ageless elves, almost saints.
Darkness of war like a black cloak overshadowing all things
Squelching light, hope, life.
But its reign only brief until
Hearts are changed; weapons turned to ploughshares.
Through darkness, a light;

A green leaf pushing through scorched wasteland.
This life of pain, great suffering
A gray tumultuous storm,
Soon to pass.

His deep, rich imagination
Almost deifying nature,
But really, seeing God as all in all.
Transfiguring.

## Friendship

The hermit in the cave
desert father, desert mother
solitude, friendship with God.

But the hermit in the desert of modernity
suffers similarly, but isolation almost desolation
leads to despair.
Pray for consolation. Yet pray for desolation to keep humble.
The Jesuit paradox.

Friendship the buoy
uplifting, edifying to keep from suicidal loneliness.
The modern malaise afflicting a collective, a culture
lost and uncertain. Seeking positivity in the midst of a cruel world.

Tolkien hobbits, elves, dwarfs, men, wizards: exemplify camaraderie,
collegiality—
friendship bringing each through catastrophe to see the eucatastrophe.
Christ, the friend to the apostles that commissioned them, like brothers
to set the world afire.
Friendship: the quality bringing us through a dark world,
through suffering in the trenches—keeping each other alive.

Each knows something the other does not.
Iron sharpening iron.
This uncertain, painful world—
a desire to isolate from the pain,
but the friend pulls one out of the self,
small community edifying and bringing health and light
to the blindness, short-sightedness of the individual.
Friendship needed more now, possibly than ever.

The cure for pain: God-ordained

friendship.

## Ice

In this winter melancholy

the deep rumble of ice cracking beneath my feet is needed;

like thunder rumbling in the distance, a dark, frozen scape with a white jagged line running along the clear frozen water.

Snow a white down upon forest floor, powder upon the trees,

twigs snapping under frigid weight.

Birds dancing, hopping—a red cardinal contrasted against pure white.

The silence of the wood

snow a curtain dampening noise of human toil.

Rabbit tracks, like a path to follow imprinted upon hoary frost.

White, blue icicles hang from rocks where little waterfalls fell in the thaw.

Arctic air, clear atmosphere

where black dome reveals the speckled stars, ice in their seemingly cold distance. Painting pictures in the black sky.

Snow crunching beneath booted feet. Hearing the icy cold.

Sun rises in arctic air,

ice illumines like fire, the snowy fields brighter than the whitest tunic transfigured.

## December 2nd

Colony of bees

grumpy on cloudy day

fifty-pounds honey stored

survive dark winter—sweet honeycomb

each bee

humility—its place, purpose known.

Advent candle burns

awaiting His return—

love incarnate.

Hive of humanity disordered.

Bloody host raised

becalming, calling

us to His cross—

His humility—

His saving grace.

## December 23rd

Holly branch, evergreen
Seed buried beneath
frozen ground.
Incarnate theanthropos
born beneath the earth
from womb—consuming fire,
yet not consumed.
Bodies in graves like seeds.
Incarnate God
redeemed mankind
by becoming flesh
dying then rising again
raising mankind with Him.

Holly branch evergreen
symbol of eternity.

## Winter Wonder

Cold, clear air
clear, dark sky.
Ice-pick stars in the black dome.
Crescent moon bright,
the face of grace.

A blazing red cardinal amidst white and ice
ice-encapsulated branches
preserved and beautiful
awaiting the thaw for little green buds.

String of lights
emblazoning the light of the world.
Decorous trees, lighted mangers
awaiting the King.

January and February dark, dismal
crippled in despair.
To see sacramental beauty is paramount in this season.
Gift me the grace to always see.

## Ash Wednesday

In cold winter we die.

Dust to dust our ash spread upon the forehead.
One day we will die, the winter of our lives.

Mortal, imperfect, unworthy.
But only say the word . . .
My soul, my soul
what dry bones can live again?

Remembrance of sin; its awful destructive force.
But after winter's chill, comes spring.
Only say the word and my soul shall be healed.

Paramore discarded, lies silenced, hurtful words shut, secrets confessed
Lent, a turning from one's natural destructive intent.
Grace given to be more like the only perfect person,
Resurrected ages ago.

The breath still stirs the air and brings new life,
when we accept it and welcome
the breeze and fire of comfort and truth.
Love divine that transforms the hardened heart to live again.
Forgive the trespass of heart and will;
and forgive other's trespasses . . . that destroy the mind and the will.

Pray for us sinners now and the hour of death.
The ash upon forehead reminds we are but a vapor given an allotted time;
to live it well and strive for goodness.
What a mess of things one can create . . .

But God's grace waits at the next breath to turn the will back toward Himself,
who is life and peace.
In the resurrection of all things, we live again. From ash to newness of life.

## St. George's Day

Blood-red rose cut;
stalk of wheat.
Dragons slain,
resurrection—a dead kernel falling to the ground.

Dragon's blood births a rose,
red, red rose
our passion, our slain sin budding a rose:
life and thorns, through pain;
we resurrected.
Our passions transformed from worship of idols to the passion and worship of Christ.
The lance pierced Christ's side, renewing us in water and blood.

Fallen to the ground we die,
a seed buried in the dust
to rise as splendid as waves of wheat bending in the wind
renewed in the breath.

Though cut from the source of giving life,
red rose dries, keeping its beauty
reminding in kernels of wheat
of dead risen;
the kingdom come—renewed earth and heaven
New Jerusalem.

## Mercy Sunday

The tomb empty,
Christ visited those
despairing,
repairing twisted, broken hearts.
Wounds in hands; side
present
presenting new body
his wounds to heal ours.

His shalom
burns joy within broken image
making whole
by body, blood, mercy
remission.
Permission to enter the
kingdom by his side
through the cross
to newness of life
bodily resurrected
in mercy and grace
to see his face
shine upon our countenance.

Yet, my heart still aches.

## Trinity Sunday

I waded in the river,
the current pulling at my legs.
The stones hurting my feet.

Holy Ghost pulling at my heart.

Love that pulls my body
in water currents
telling me to live—
be in motion
not dead and stagnant.
Love that hurts my feet
to push me onward.

The Father is God, the Son is God, the Spirit is God, but one is not the other.

The river flows on
conjunction with time
Trinity in time and outside of
it is in rhyme
with the river.
This Love incarnation—all things might be redeemed.
This Love not contained in one thing
but its mark in all
will bring this good creation
conjoining with eternity.
The river will flow on
pain gone
resistance distant
memory—
no more.

Water of river and ocean
and mountain stream
will wash us clean
only good remaining
with us in eternity.

## Babylon Forgotten

Exiled in Babylon,
Jerusalem forgotten
its hills, forests, menagerie of beasts and birds . . .
the beauty of the Mediterranean
and warm, balmy breeze . . .
the Galilean shores to the north
the heights—reaching toward
the heavens.

The arid desert with mineral
waters receding, yet healing.
Rushing waters, rivers pure.
Cleansing, washing clean.
O Jerusalem, I have not forgotten.
Mother; home. A healing to the soul.
The Gadarene swine have drowned.
The desert land—wandering
remembering glimpses of home.
The mists on the water.
Palm and olive and acacia.
White stone wall.

Heart in exile
longs for home.

Jezreel Valley fertile
awaits clash of nations
clash of human wills and its desire
in opposition to God's.
The Mount of Transfiguration,
the Mount of Temptation,
Mount of Olives
agony and burden—
heavyhearted nearing
death.

The hard wood and the
blood.
The olive press—
tremendous agonizing,
crushing weight.
Dark clouds,
blood moon
sky cracked—earth rent.

Exiles return—come home
the twelve gates open
rest from your weary journey
upon desert and arid climes.
Rocky paths and rutted earth.
From loss of soul
and broken spirit;
a funereal mind.
Rest from the weeping in the night;
bitter loneliness . . .
Sleep in the arms of beloved
Jerusalem.
Babylon forgotten.

## untitled

I don't believe in an upstairs downstairs understanding of heaven.

More like a marriage that will one day be.

A renewing of all things material and spiritual—the two realities merging present.

Christ, the incarnate reality of what is to come.

Love, beautiful without pain.

Death, the vanquished enemy.

## Remember in the Light of Your Love

"Remember me in the light of your love,"
golden sun, pour your light upon wretched soul;
grace illuminate to move in love,
peace as the dove descending
upending the world in grace and light.
I wait upon the Lord in stillness
trembling to hear your voice to alight
a dim soul with fire, grace, illuminating.

A storm rumbles in the distance, black cloud,
Lightning erupting, flashes of luminescence
Rain pouring, battering the wretched soul.
The Nazarene walking upon water
calming the sea and storm to offer grace
to the drowning wretched soul pummeled by grace.

## Silence

Always saying a prayer
coming and going
for sons and daughters
friends and enemies.
Touching the doorpost
where blood once painted the frame.
A prayer for the innocent and the lost.
Every breath
Shaping the day of things unseen.
A child's laugh:
a prayer of joy.
Tears: a prayer of grief
acquiescence and relinquishment.
Silence:
a prayer of rest.
In silence to behold
Thy glory.

## beauty

beauty in the mind,

beauty divine.

The subjective–matter of taste

beauty leading toward truth, toward goodness

beauty for its own sake,

leading toward lust or idol worship,

but beauty has grace

to illuminate

to transform.

# Foxes

Foxes in the garden
tearing the ground
eviscerating fruit of earth
roots torn, bulbs ripped from fertile ground.
Smell of blood in the black soil;
the tail brushing the ground.
Teeth tearing; paws digging.

Broken boundaries
violated trust.

Fence posts driven into the ground
wire put in place
gardens tilled; replanted;
raised beds.
Blackened soil; seeds planted
green gently peeking from the rich earth.
Soon to bud and bloom
in beauty—
Apollonian order;
Dionysian chaos kept at bay—
until uprooting and resurrection needed.

Disrupting foxes kept out;
no digging allowed;
rifle kept close to deter ruining critter.

# Pearl

I had a pearl of great worth.
I put it in a box—hid it away.
Too dangerous to let anyone know about it.
It was worth too much.
It's beauty radiant, dangerous.

I lived a mundane life,
only I knew the secret of this pearl.
Still hidden, I hid it from friends, family, all who knew me.
Years went by, and I forgot about the pearl.
Loss and death overwhelmed me with grief.
I forgot about the pearl of great price.

The pearl forgotten,
studies and a shaky purpose took its place.
Something I thought I wanted.
That too burned–went up in flame.
Burning down the house.

In the ashes I found the pearl.
But blamed all upon the perfect milky sphere.
I gave it away—to the depths of the earth.
A weight lifted.
I was freed.

I met another, to share joy with.
But became a slave.
Though I gave the pearl away,
all I ever sought was that very same perfect milky sphere.

So went on a quest to find what I gave away.
Everywhere I looked I saw a glimpse of the perfect milky sphere.
But none of it was the pearl itself.
It wasn't in the cloud cover;
wasn't in the mountains;

not the ocean depths;
not in the sand or the sea;
neither the grassy valley nor the country field.
Not in the eyes of the beauty.
Or in all the knowledge in the world.

A man of wisdom told me, it was nearer me than my very heartbeat,
but further than the farthest star.
I looked to the heavens, to the darkest star—
within myself.
But it wasn't there either.

I looked everywhere.
I never found it again.
Until one evening, on my deathbed—

I saw it.
And I lived again.

## Upside Down

Positivism turned on its head
twentieth century a centennial of death;
twenty-first began in death and destruction.
A Dionysian world we live in.

Jansenism, Calvinism deterministic
see humans fully depraved
unable to do or make any good.

But the image of God is paradox
still burning within—
though dimmed by concupiscence,
will to power, greed, disordered loves.

The prodigal son
Mary of Magdelaine;
David; Jacob; Cain;
we, human, mixture of good and evil.
Goodness certainly an end when aiming toward Good;
Evil always capable of when aiming toward ourselves.

Jansenism; Positivism; Pessimism; Optimism;
Gnosticism; Nihilism;
Epicurean;
none explain or suffice or bring levity.
Longing within rarely satiated,
but the end of our aim: the ground of our being.

Our self-destruction will end us and others;
But His resurrection and grace will save us—
because He created Good.
In the beginning was the Logos and the Word became flesh.
Created things not inherently evil;
We fell, yes, corrupt.

But redemption is nigh.
The world turned on its head—a reversal begun
and continues to refresh all flesh.
By grace of turning one's gaze back to the Father
who opens arms in welcome; in all weather.

### Jewel

Ornate interior, illumined candles,
gilded cross, richly painted icons.
Plain, rough stone exterior.
Interior person in contemplation, prayer, obedience by grace to God.
Jewels within our plain exterior.
Illumined habits, lit candles within.
Countenance alight, bringing the soul to brightness and rich color—
deep blues, blood reds, gold.
Christ a fire burning us clean, bringing blood to our cheeks,
color and light to our countenance.

### Icons

Shadows of the divine
Copies to remind,
Focus the will
To meditate
On grace.

Crucifix:
Body slain
Man-God meeting
Redeeming.
Precise pictures
Proclaiming truth.
Making God present
Through remembrance,
Transcending time,
Transcending space.

Cross upon a spire
Raising eyes toward heaven.

Do not proclaim
To shame your brother
As though icons be idols.
All is image
Which we cannot escape.
The God in all
Will not claim one thing,
But speak through all.

## Dusk

The dusky night
of blues blending with orange and pink
as the sun sets
beneath the mountains.
Saturn rises
its frosty chin glaring
twinkling through the atmosphere.
Jupiter, the King
just slipped beneath the dusky mountains
with Sol to sing a new day on the other side.
Neptune will raise his trident
sending Saturn off to sleep,
another day spent, the Last
not trumpeted forth yet.
The cosmos spins its course,
keeping time.
The curse that ages all things.

Youth is not the answer; age isn't either.
But the new day dawning on the other side.
All of creation groans for it.
The universe trembles with longing.
Longing for all things be made new.
The beginning again.
Not a cycle of life and death and life and death.
But Life in all its splendor and glory.
Saturn knows it. Awaiting the new day.

How long,
O Lord?

## Met with Joy

Let the day meet you with joy.

The ramparts we put up

to block the joy of the day.

Foundations cracked—

hearts broken,

but joy is all around us.

Breath of grace,

fill our lungs.

That we may see through

the eyes of love.

To weep at the rising of the

day—

joy and bliss.

Disc rising from the horizon

shedding light upon dimmed

countenance.

Filling us with the light of truth.

Breathe in and

Let the day meet you with joy.

## Postlude

Vision,
Dimmed by concupiscence.
A mist to fog the eyes.

A whirlwind
Never standing still,
Never at rest.

Becoming a frozen waste
Through grace
Breaking through
Frigid death
To mountain rising
An orange flame atop
Grey.

Lethe and Eunoe await
After suffering and pain
A gripping, rending grace
Beckoning soul's onward movement
Upward.

Purged, scintillating
Remaking fire.
To burst
To bloom
Like supernova
Emitting immense
Intense energy
White, azure
Blinding
Transfiguring.

"*Per correr miglior acque alza le vele/ omai la navicella del mio ingegno, che lascia dietro a se mar si crudele;/ e cantero di quel secondo regno dove l'umano spirit si purga/ e di salire al ciel diventa degno.*"

—Dante, Purgatory V.1–6

www.ingramcontent.com/pod-product-compliance
Lightning Source LLC
Chambersburg PA
CBHW070306100426
42743CB00011B/2375